PIANO SOLOS

HEART OF RED

BLOOD OF BLUE

Gated
Publishing

THE NOVEL

a girl on the run . . .
a kingdom to save

*choosing him
saves only me*

HEART OF RED
BLOOD OF BLUE

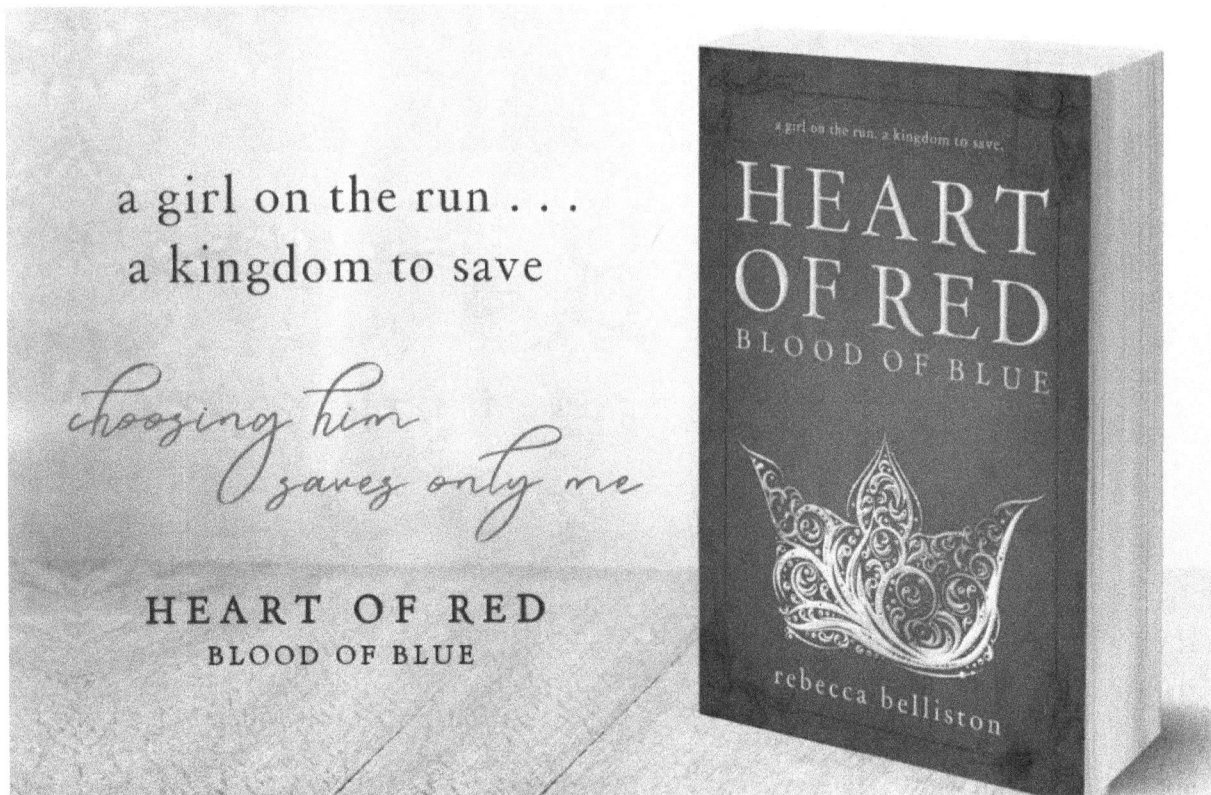

Princess Gisela of Steinland was born without color. Albino. To add to this curse, her betrothal to Prince Jerrik of Kronga ends in his death and starts a ten-year-war her father is determined to win, even if it means bringing her out of hiding to do it. Now the savage Krongon war commander, Bloodless Kristoff, seeks the hearts of the entire royal family, especially Gisela's.

Desperate, her father agrees to another alliance that involves her marrying an old brute of a king. Unwilling to be the sacrificial lamb, Gisela goes on the run. Thrown into the center of a battle between three kingdoms, she finds herself fighting for her life and the right to be truly loved.

Can the girl who started the war find a way to end it?

PRINT | EBOOK | AUDIOBOOK
rebeccabelliston.com/heart-of-red

THE BETROTHAL/JERRIK

Processional in E

Rebecca Belliston

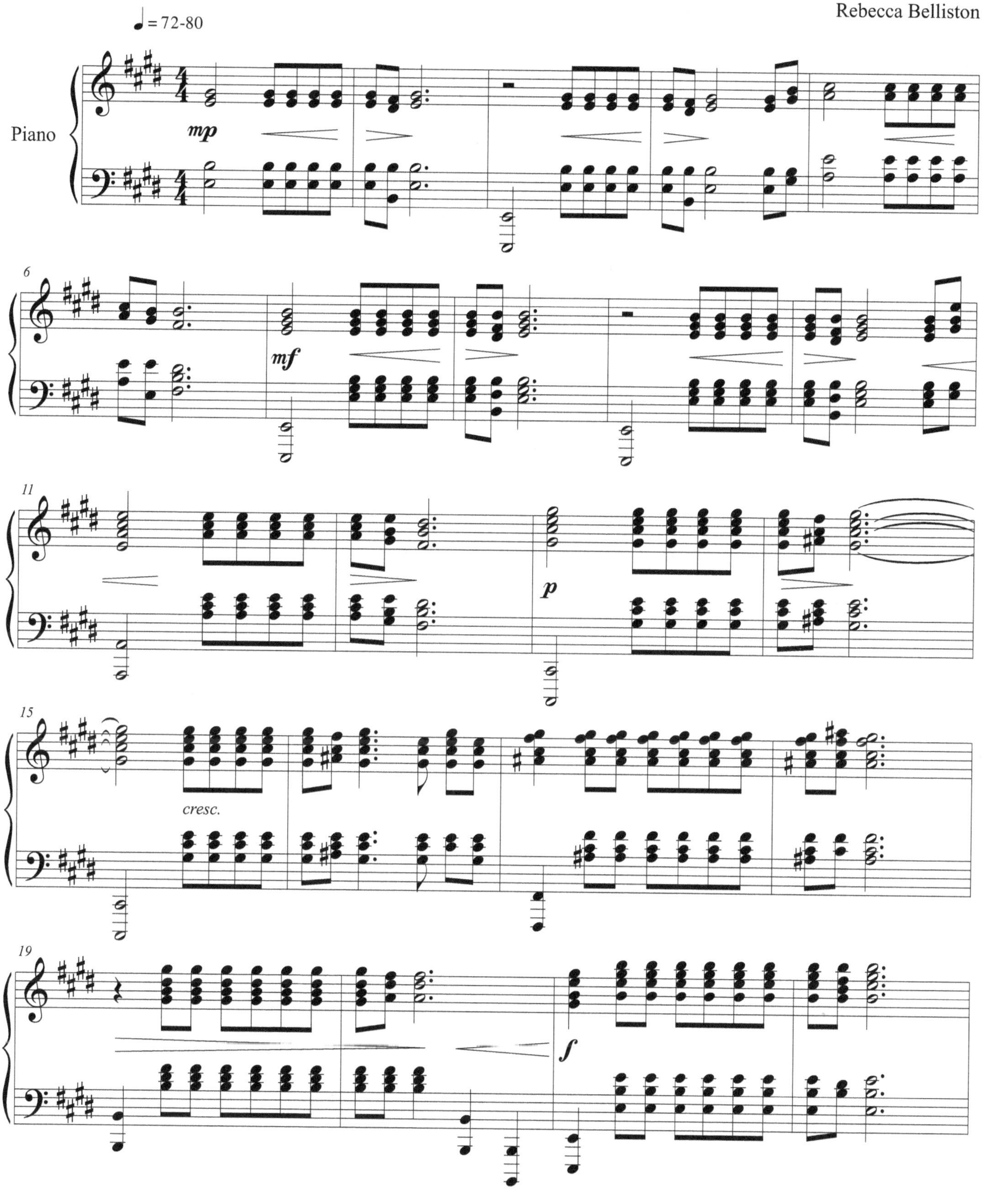

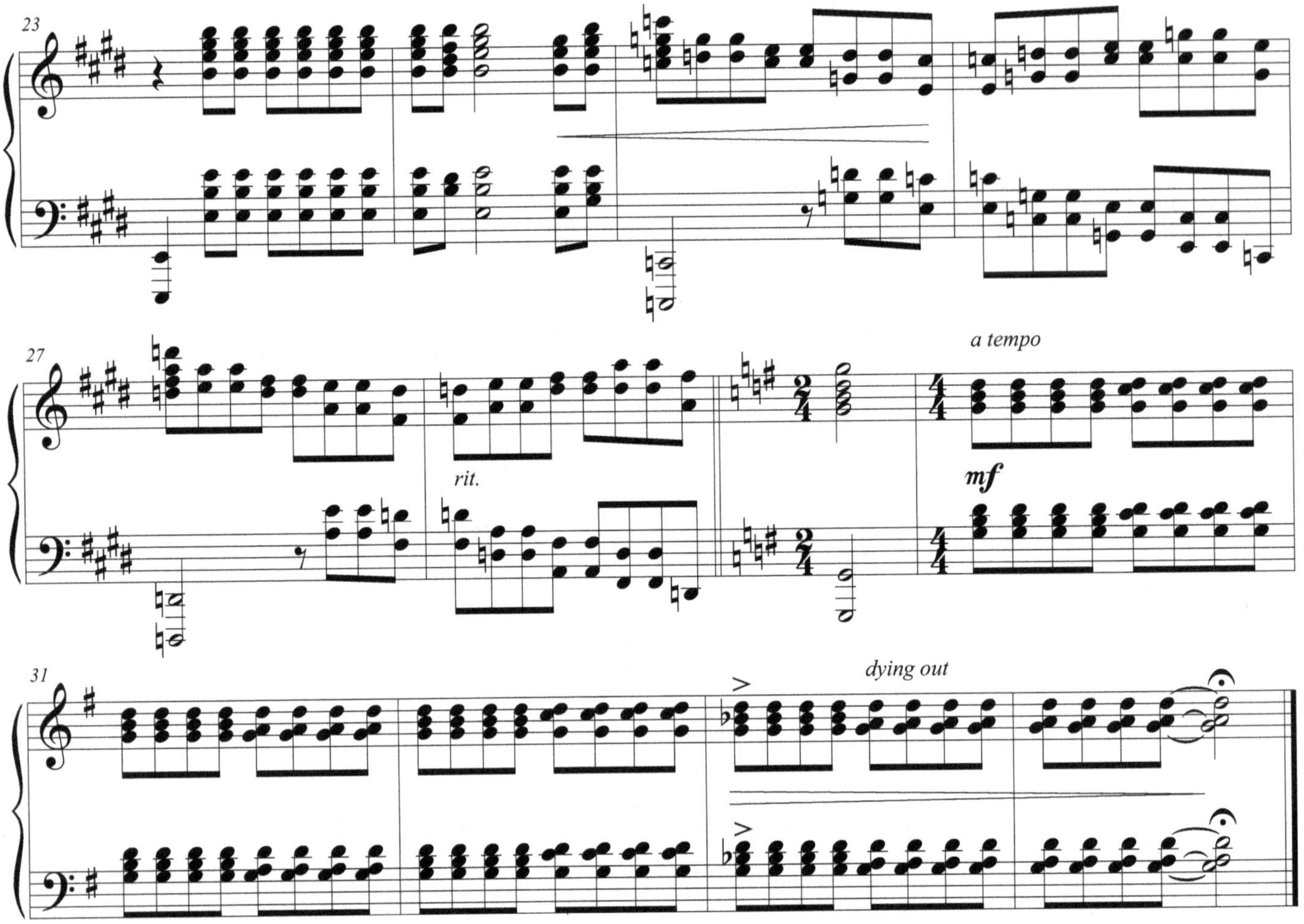
23
27
rit.
a tempo
mf
31
dying out

LEUTHAR

Prelude in C minor

Rebecca Belliston

- 4 -

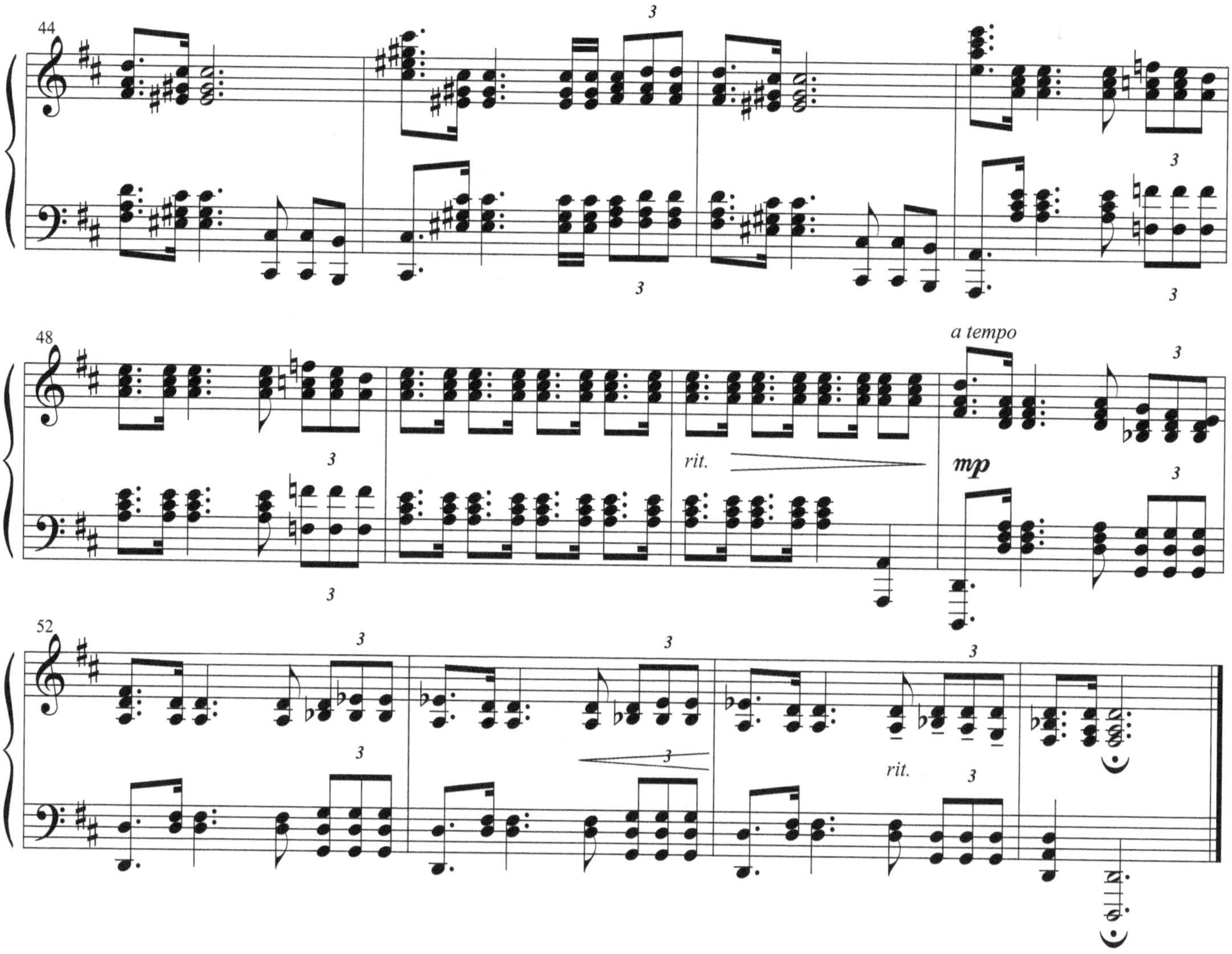
44
3
3
3
3
48
3
3
rit.
a tempo
3
mp
3
52
3
3
3
3
3
rit.
3

RYDER
Childhood Etude in Db

Rebecca Belliston

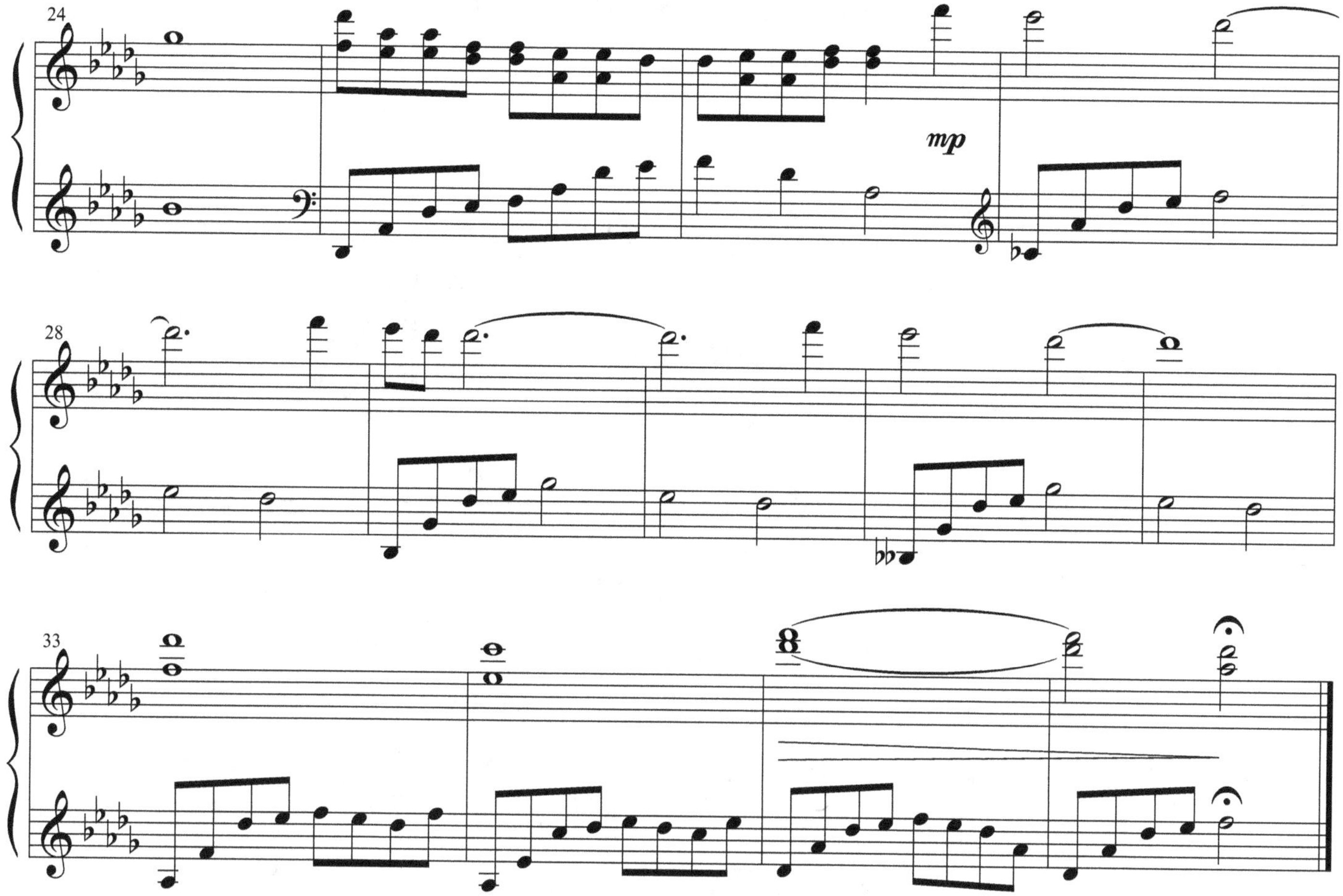
24
mp
28
33

THE SEA/SUNDET

Nocturne in D

Rebecca Belliston

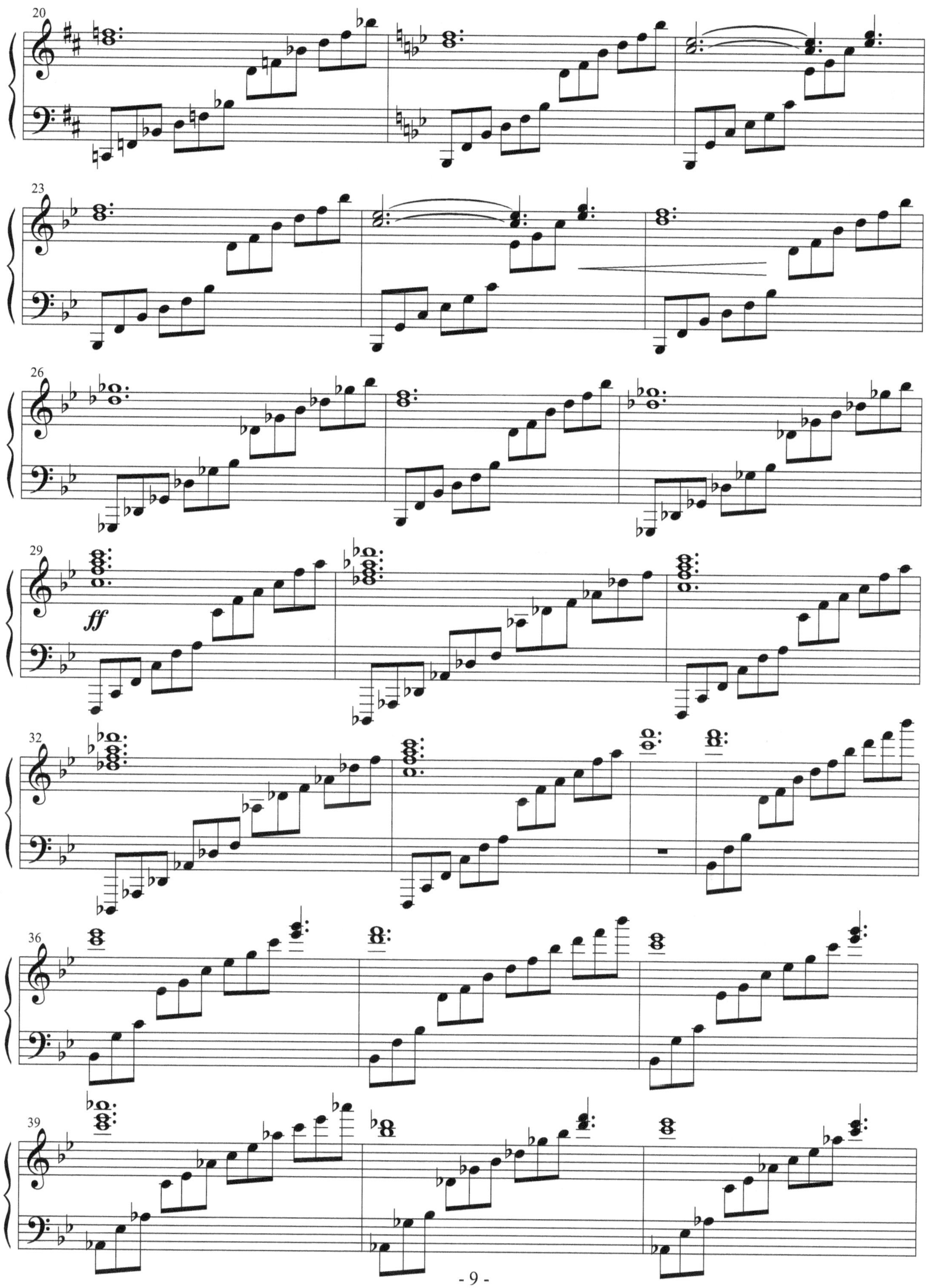
20
23
26
29
ff
32
36
39

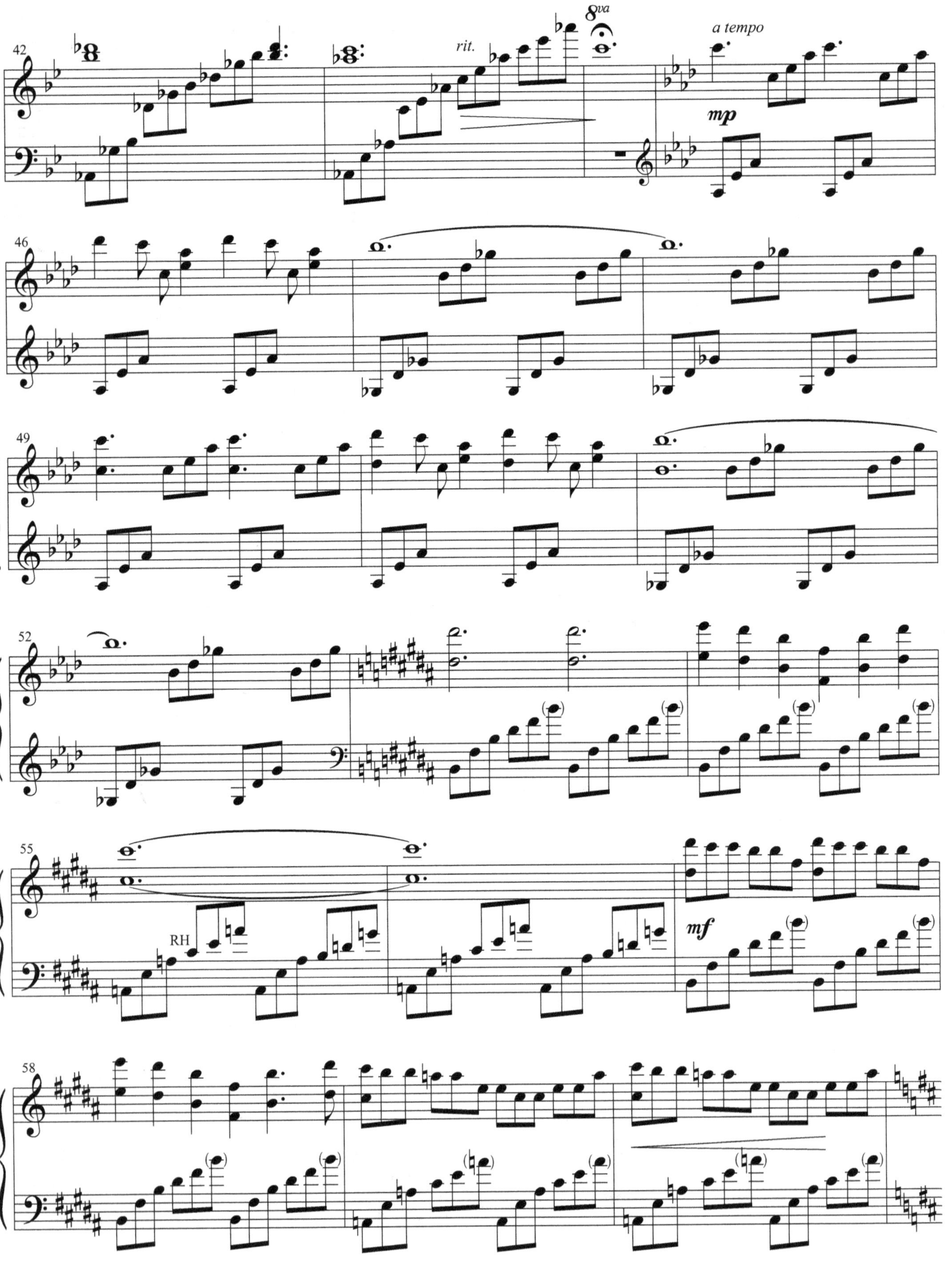

42
rit.
8va
a tempo
mp
46
49
52
55
RH
mf
58

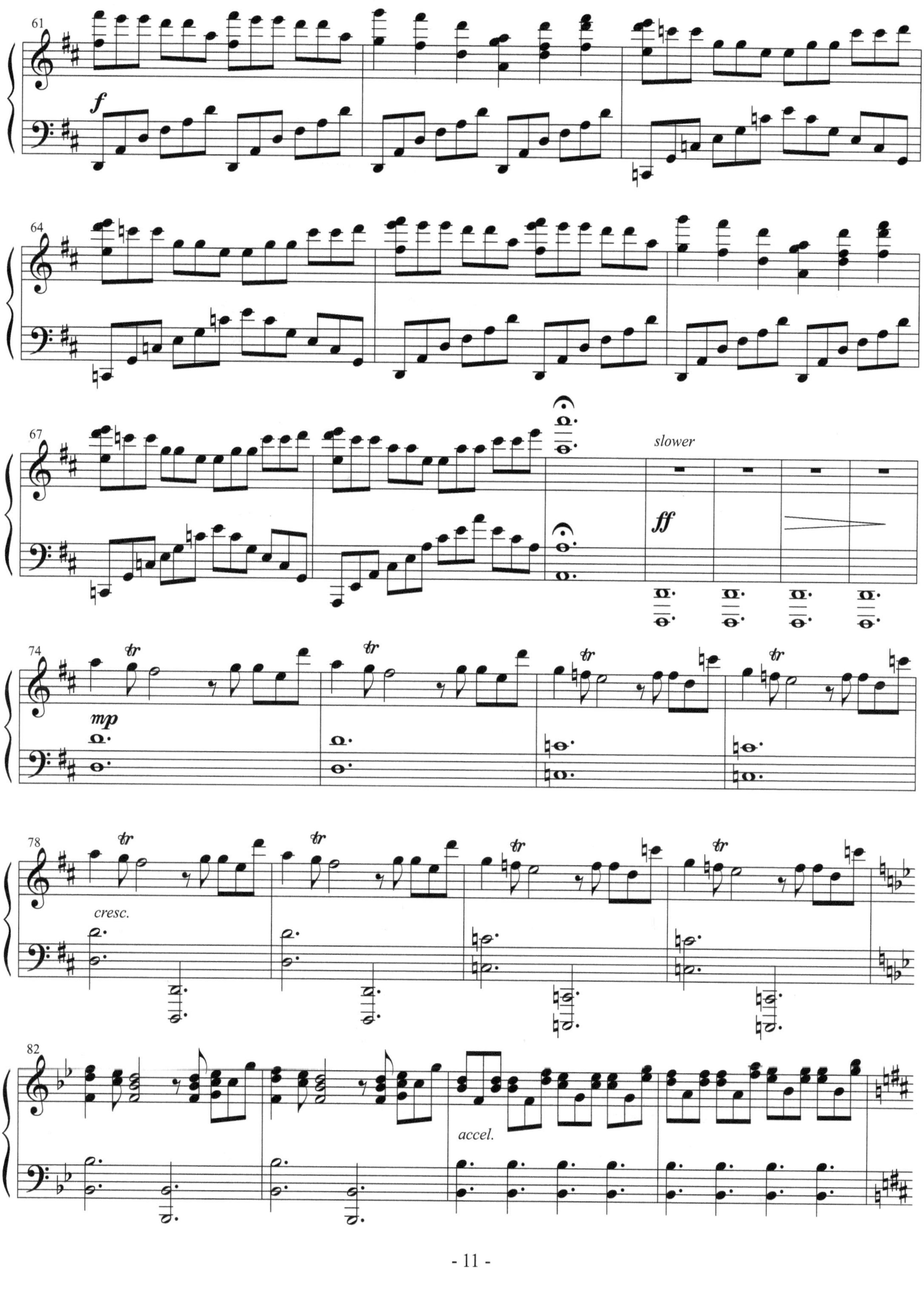
61
f
64
67
slower
ff
74
mp
78
cresc.
82
accel.

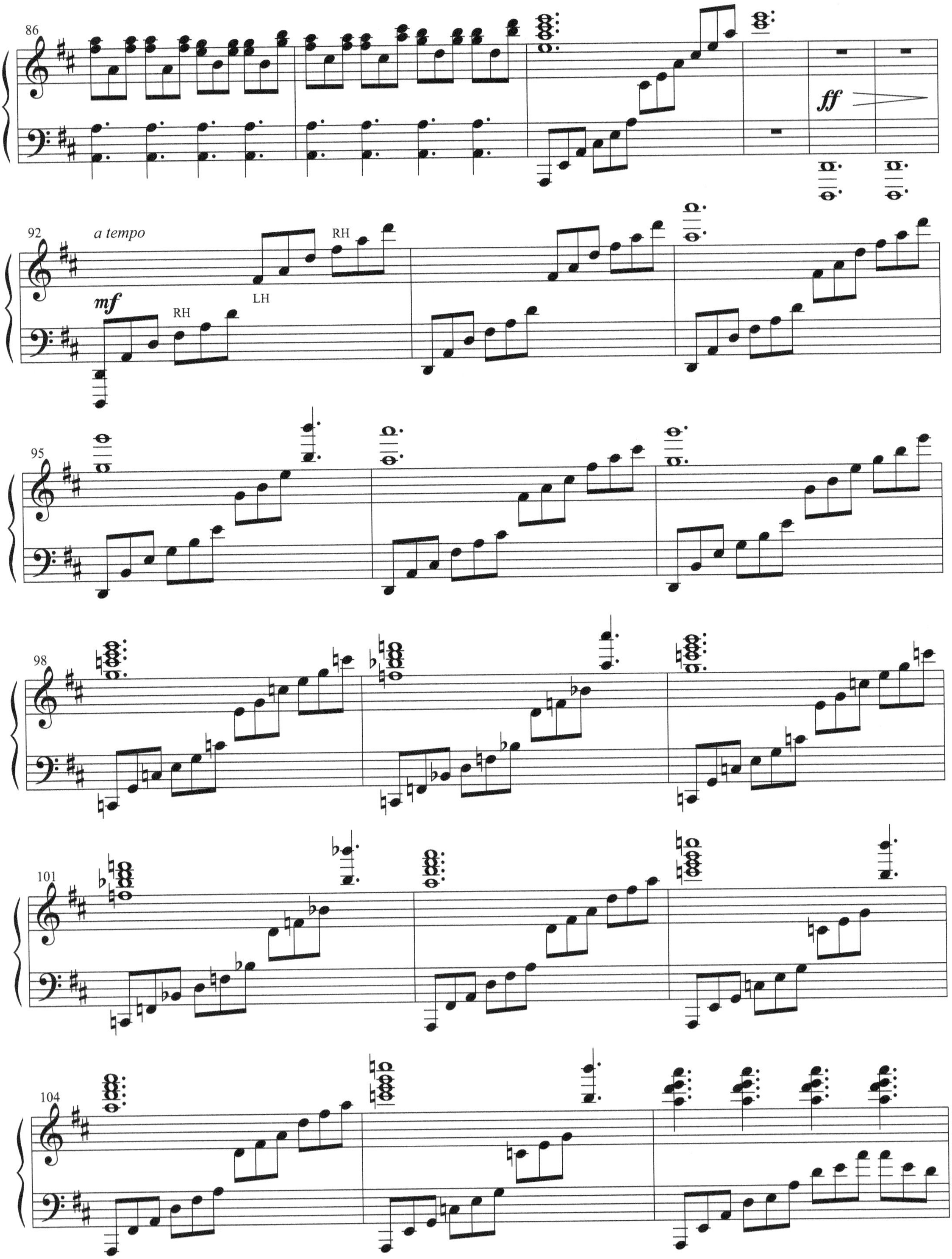
86
ff
92
a tempo
mf
RH
LH
RH
95
98
101
104

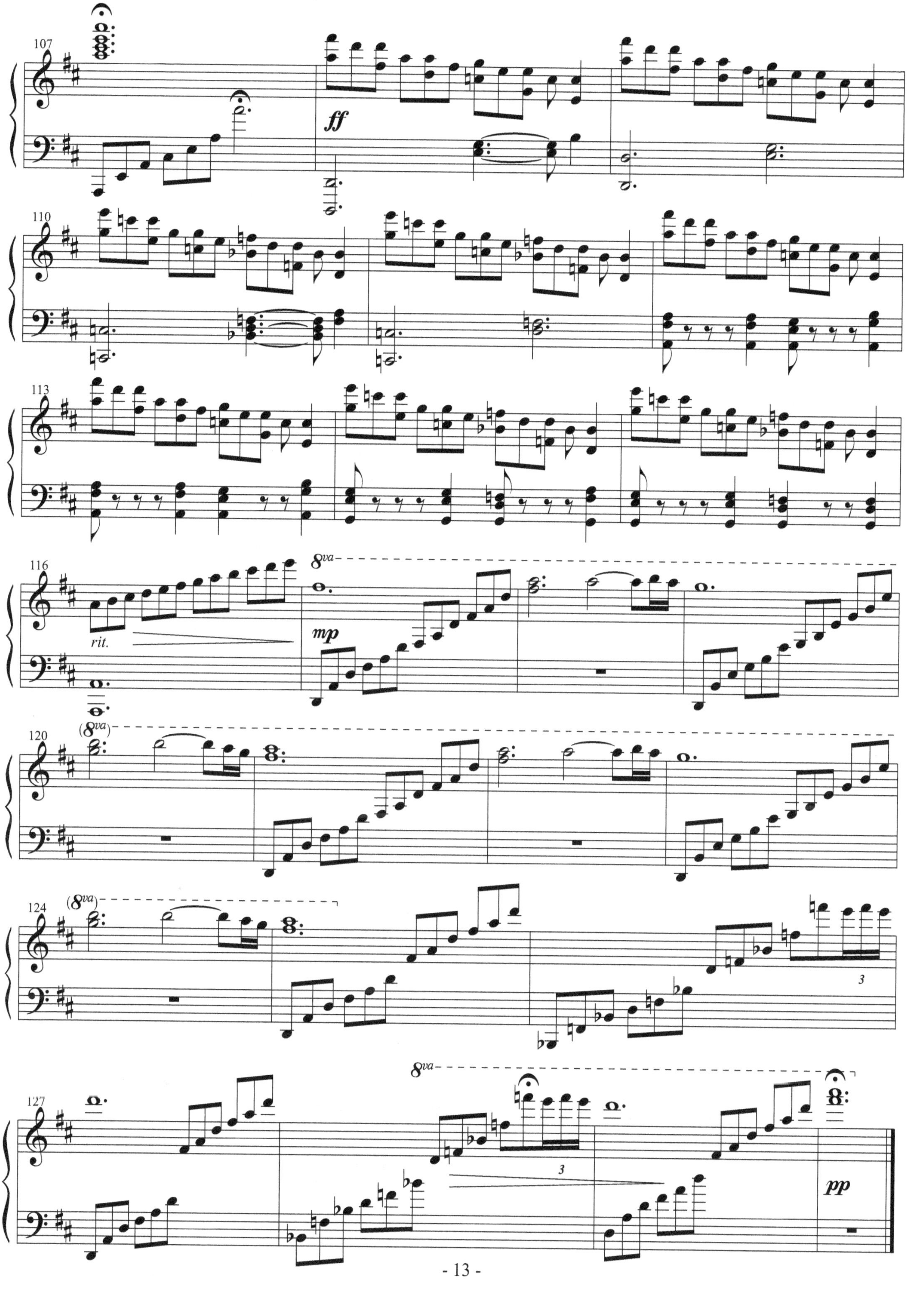
107
ff
110
113
116
rit.
8va
mp
120
(8va)
124
(8va)
3
127
8va
3
pp

THE BATTLEFIELD
Etude in C# minor

Rebecca Belliston

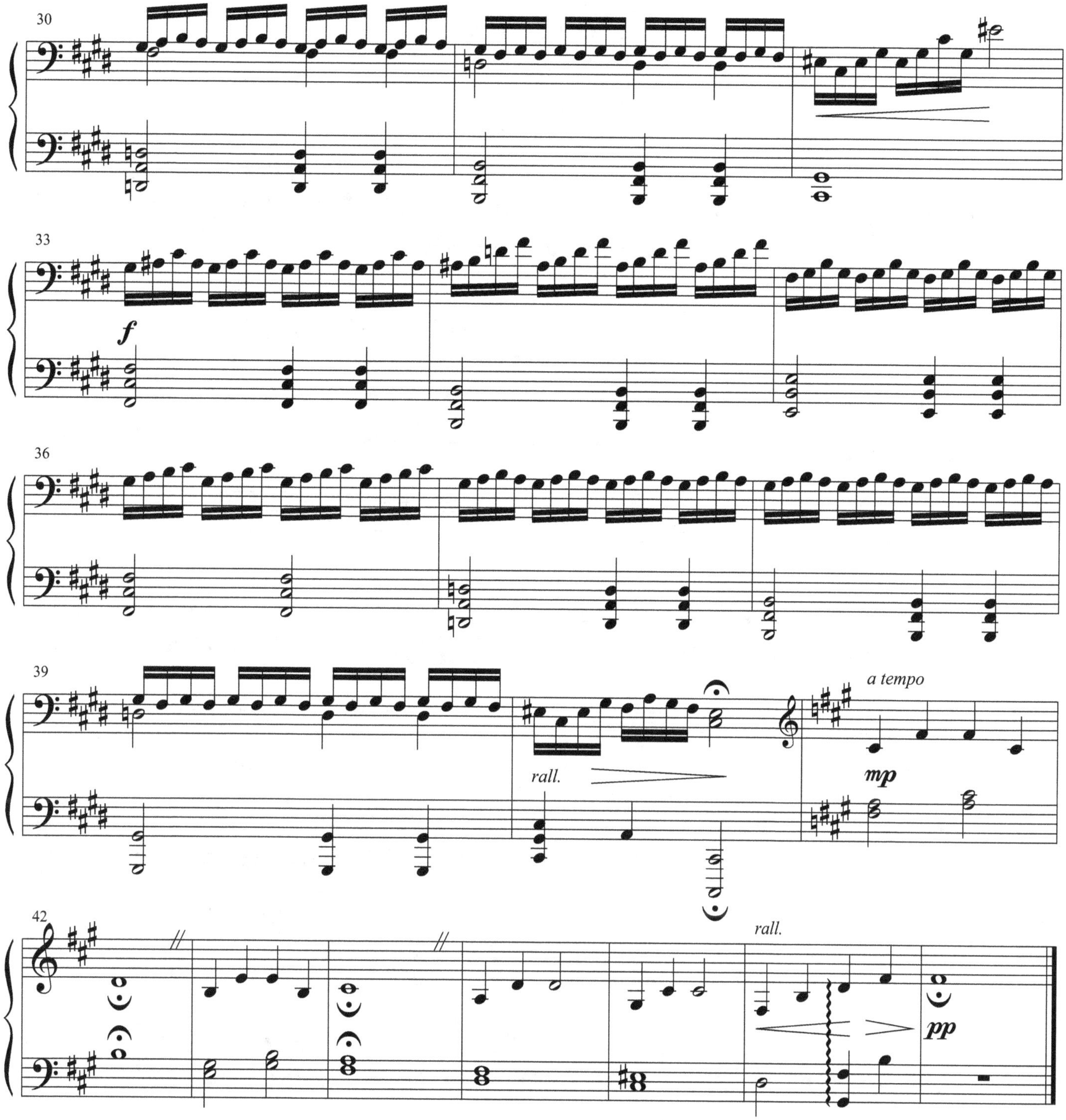
30
33
f
36
39
rall.
a tempo
mp
42
rall.
pp

VENGEANCE

Prelude in B minor

Rebecca Belliston

Somewhere in here, your right arm might start hurting. Vengeance should hurt. It's badDon't seek it in real life. However . . .
When the pain becomes too much, combine every four sixteen notes in the RH and play quarter note chords. Switch back to sixteenth notes when you can.

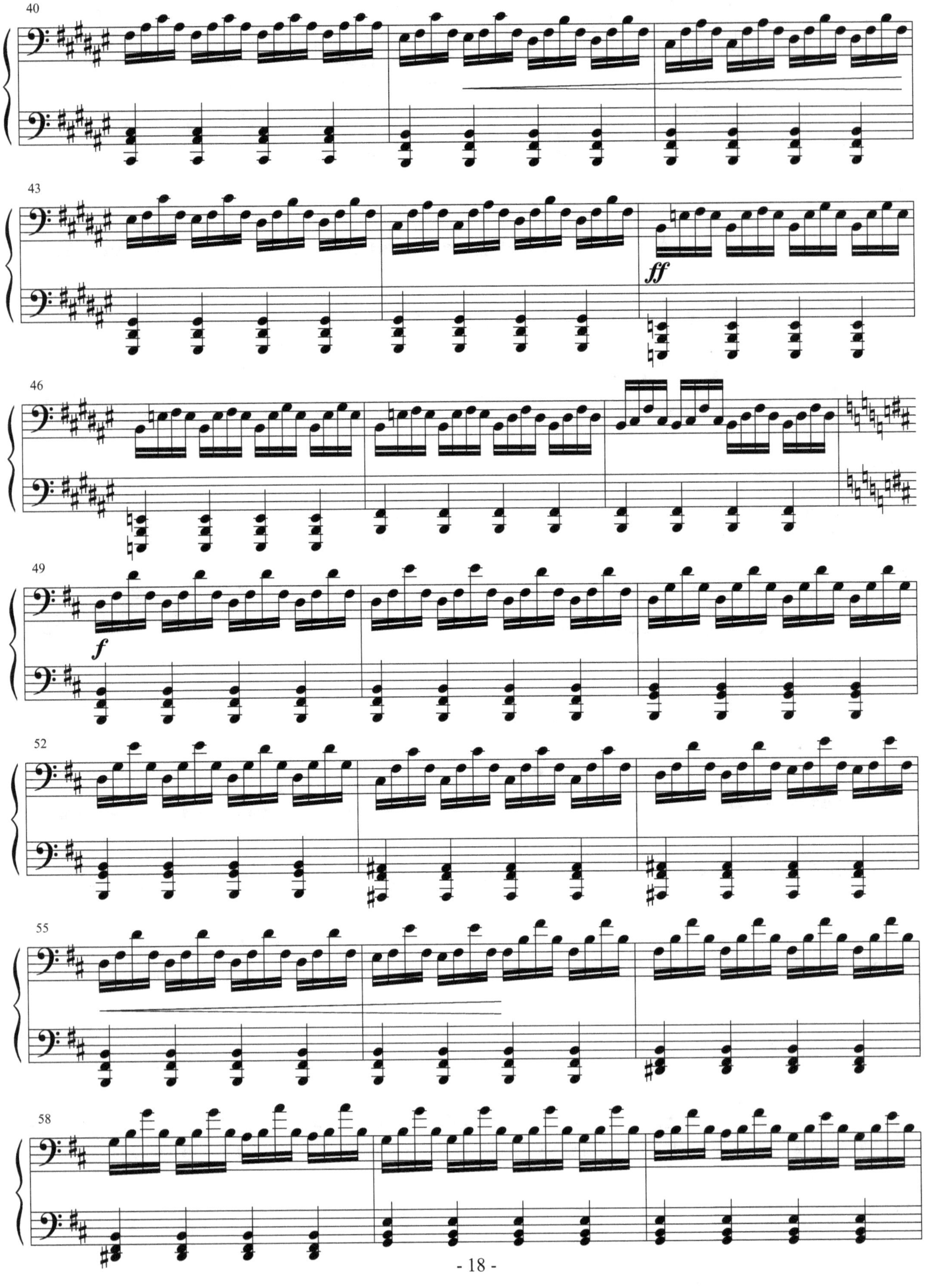
40
43
ff
46
49
f
52
55
58

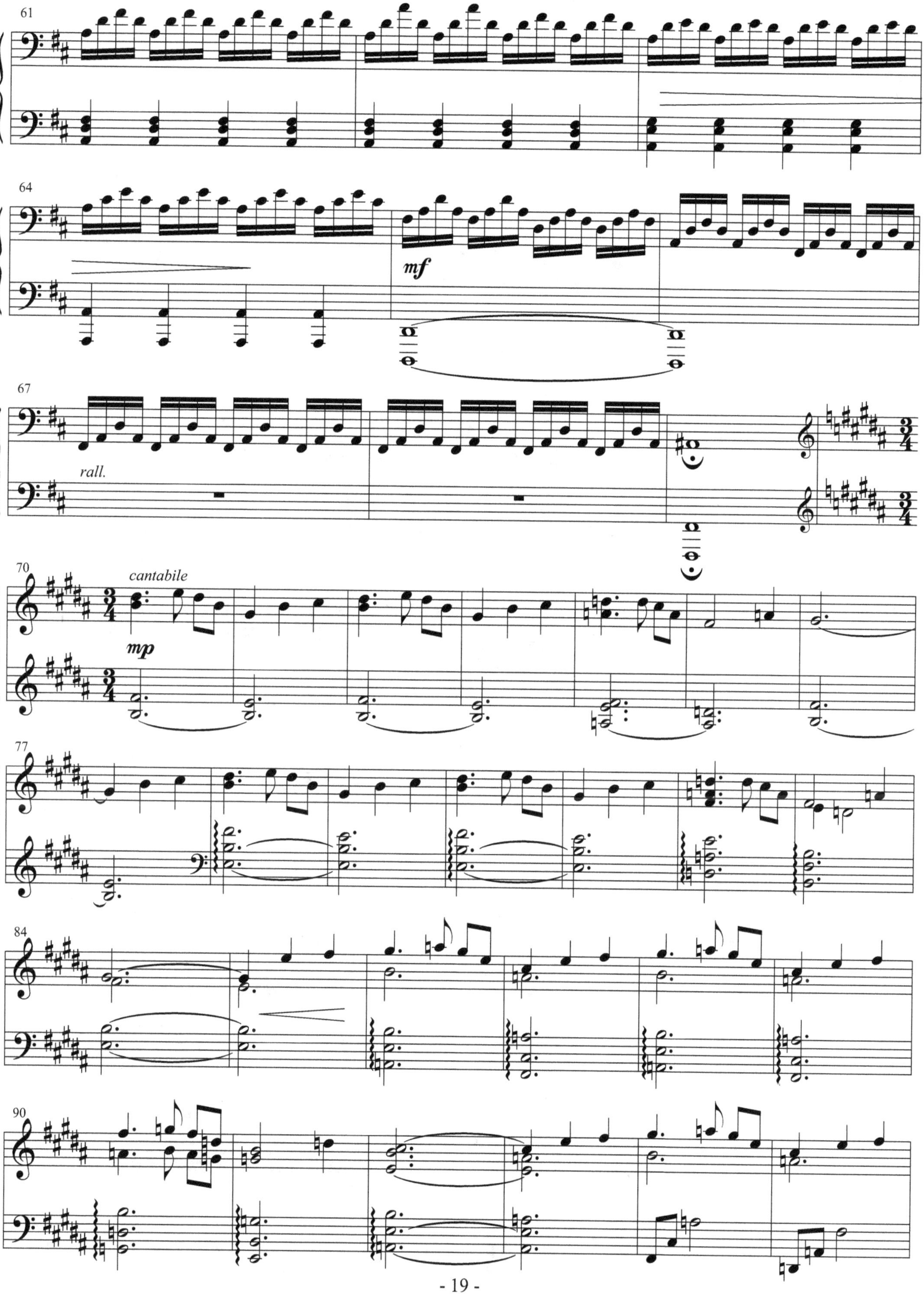
61
64
mf
67
rall.
70
cantabile
mp
77
84
90

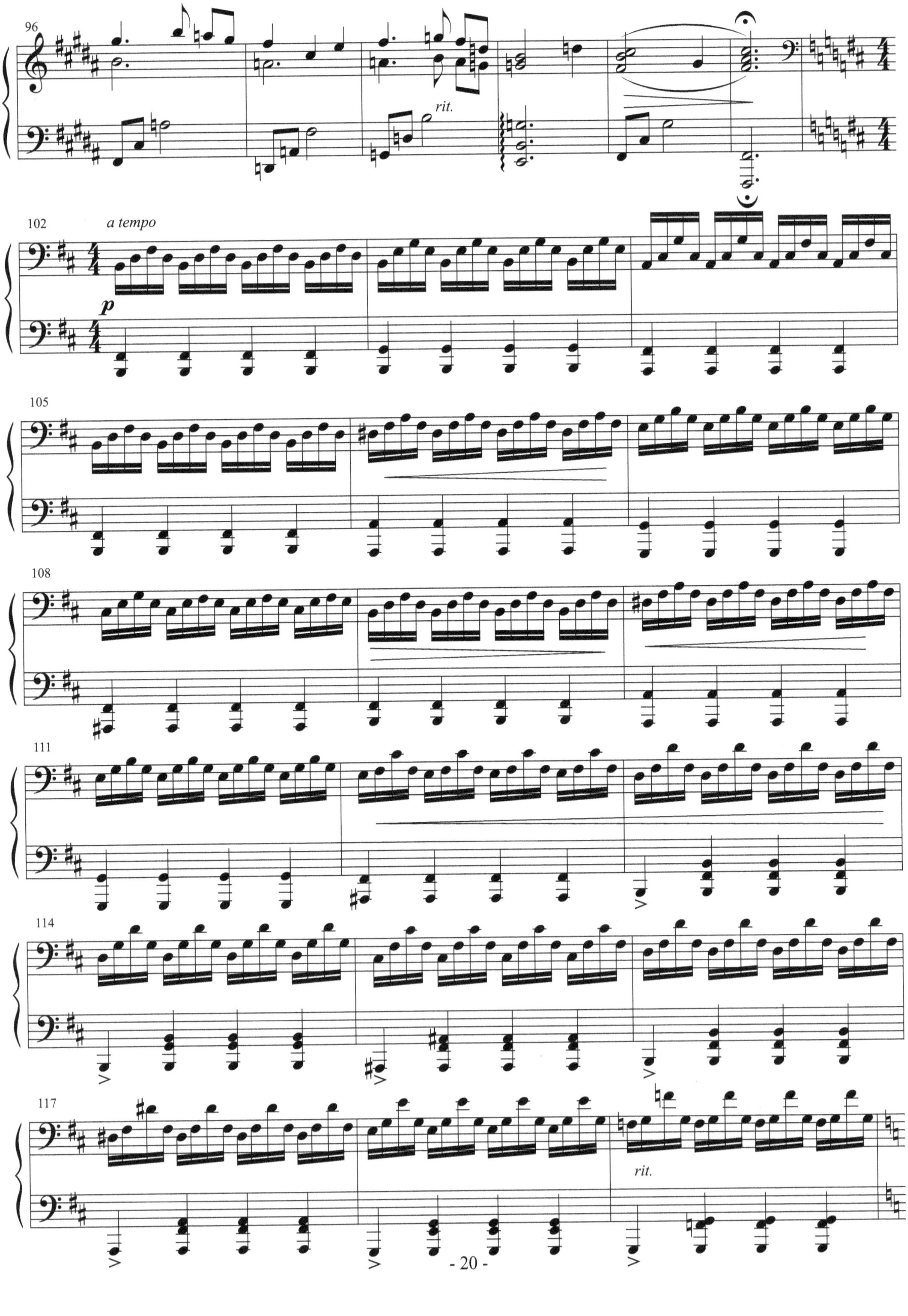
96
rit.
102
a tempo
p
105
108
111
114
117
rit.

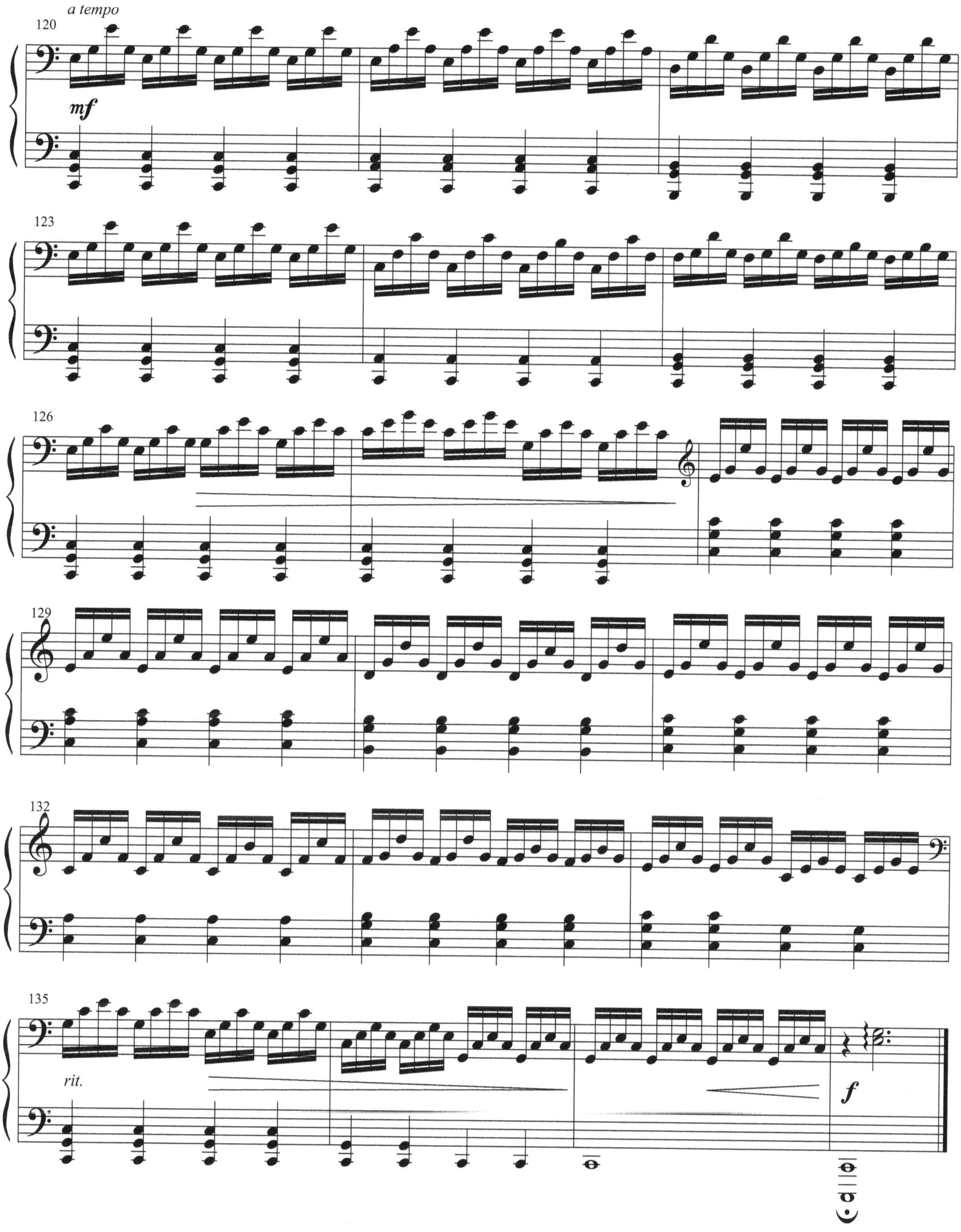
a tempo
120
mf
123
126
129
132
135
rit.
f

THE VILLAGE

Ballad in E minor

Rebecca Belliston

C/E D/F♯ G C Am B Em Em
17
Em D G/B C Em D G/B C
21
p
Em D G/B C Am D G
25
mp
Em C/E B/E Em Em C/E B/E Em
29

C D G/B C Am D G/B C
33
C/E D/F♯ G C Am B Em
37
Em D G/B C Em D G/B C
41
mp
Em D G/B C Am B E
45
rit.

THE DANCE

Jig in F

Rebecca Belliston

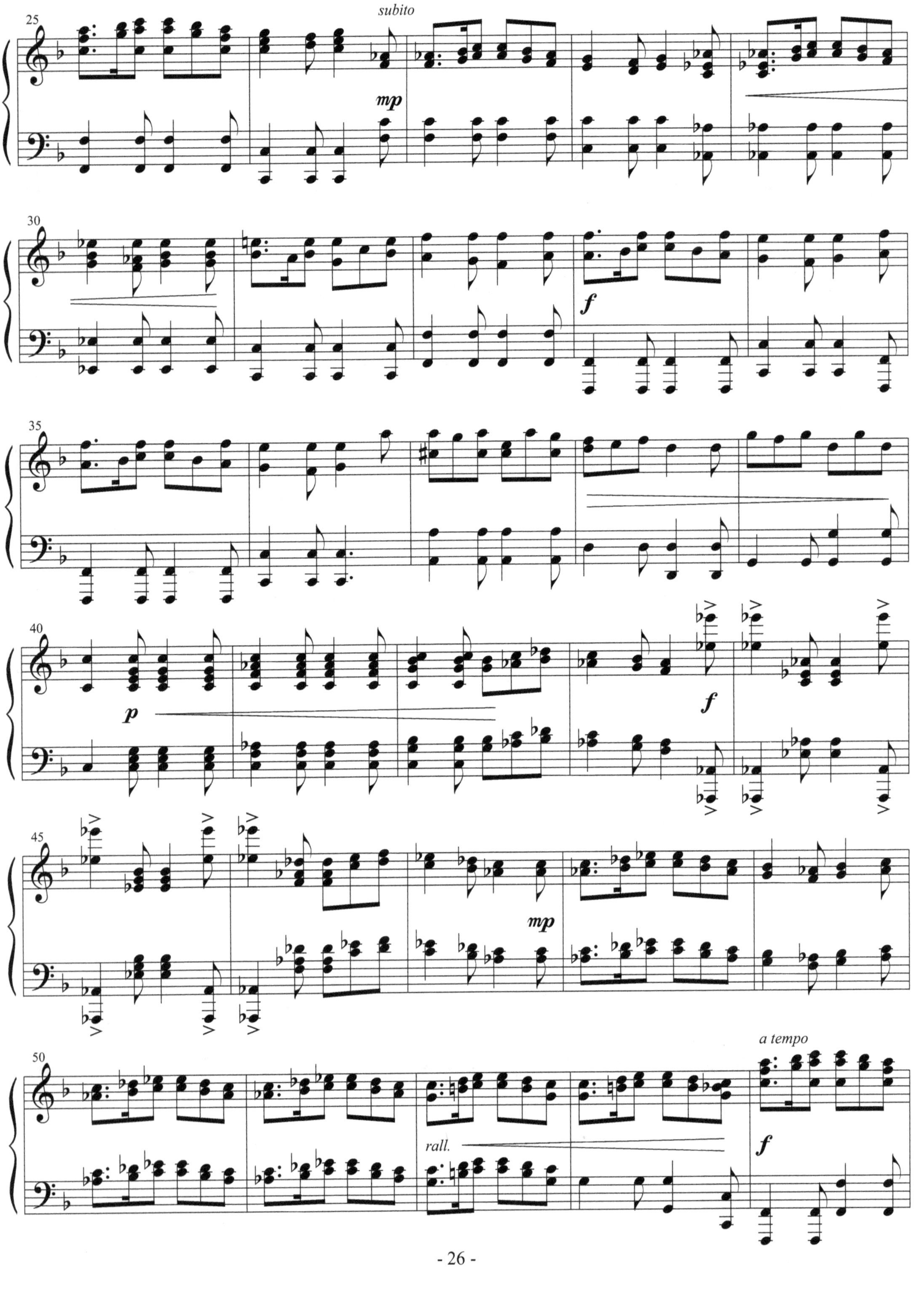
subito
mp
f
p
f
mp
a tempo
rall.
f

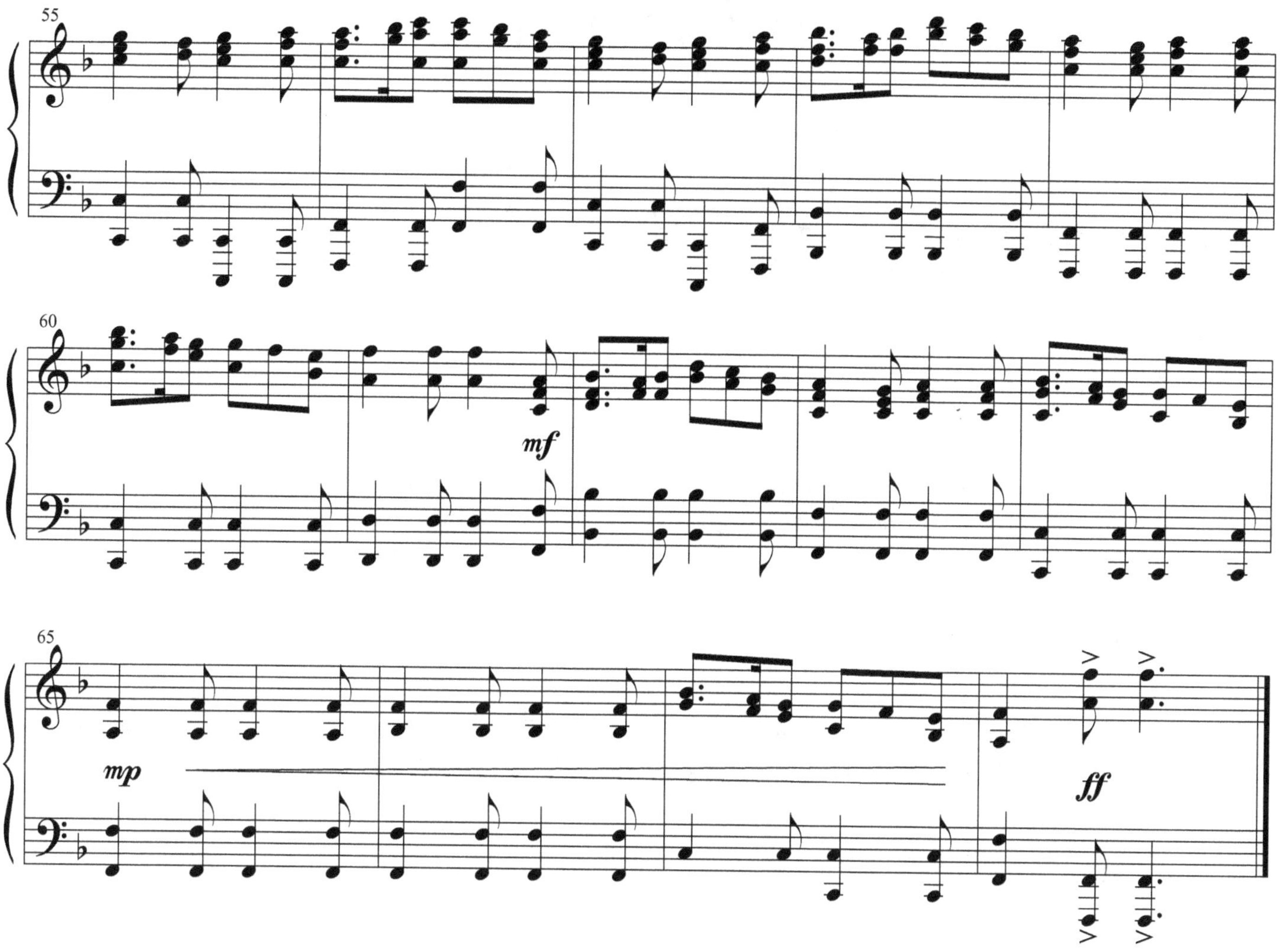
55
60
mf
65
mp
ff

TRANQUILITY
Prelude in Db

Rebecca Belliston

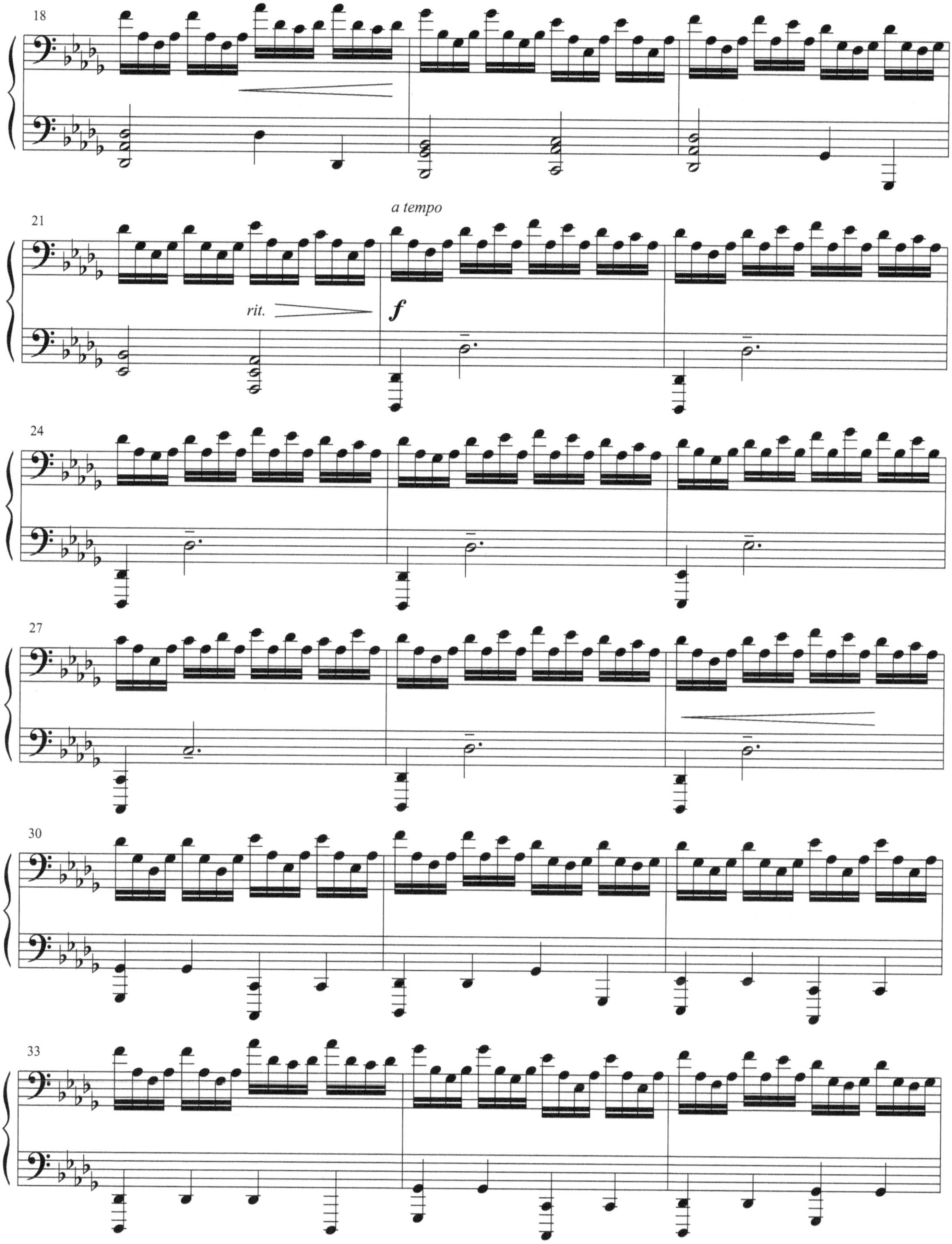
18
21
a tempo
rit.
f
24
27
30
33

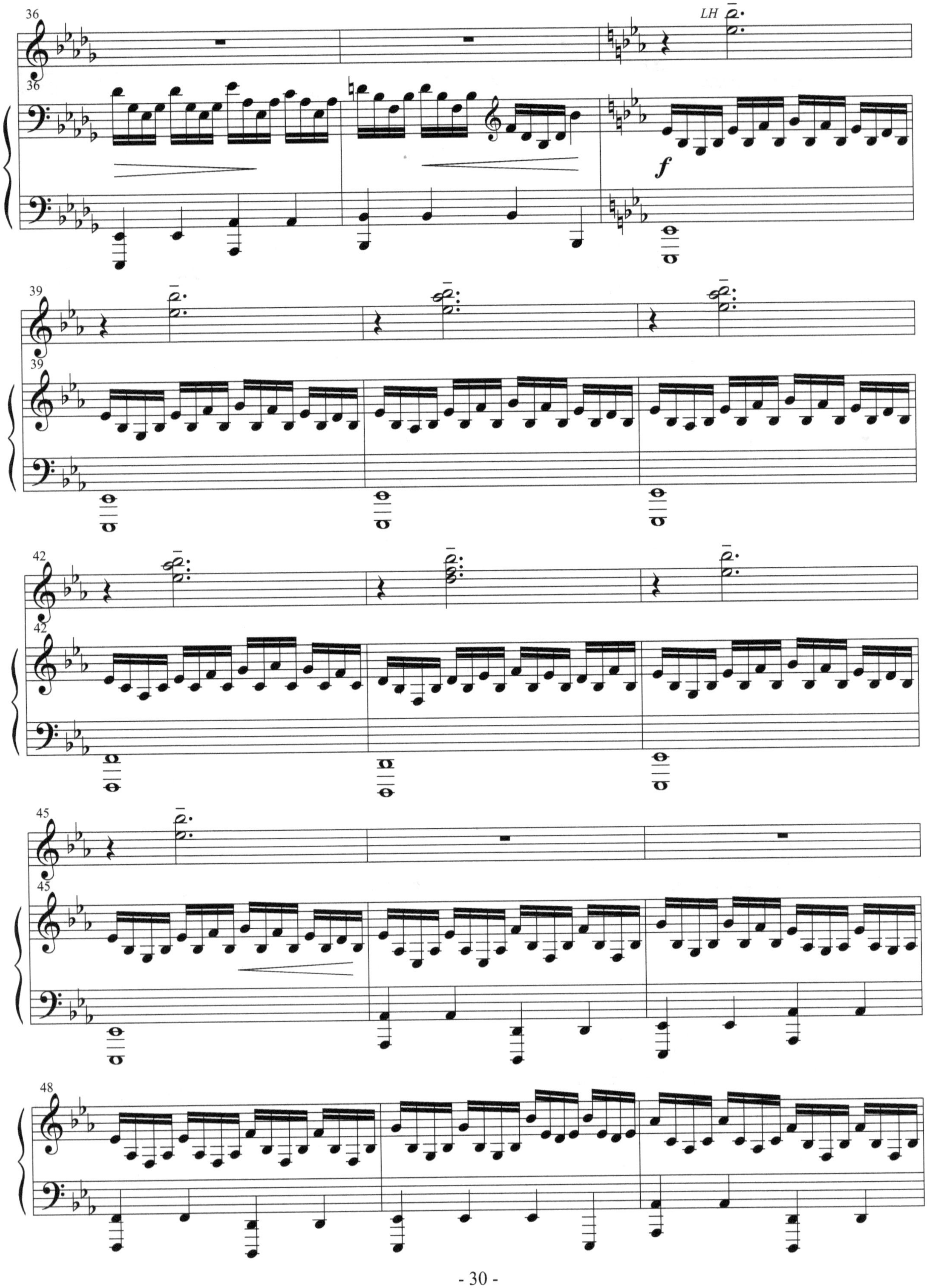
36
LH
39
42
45
48

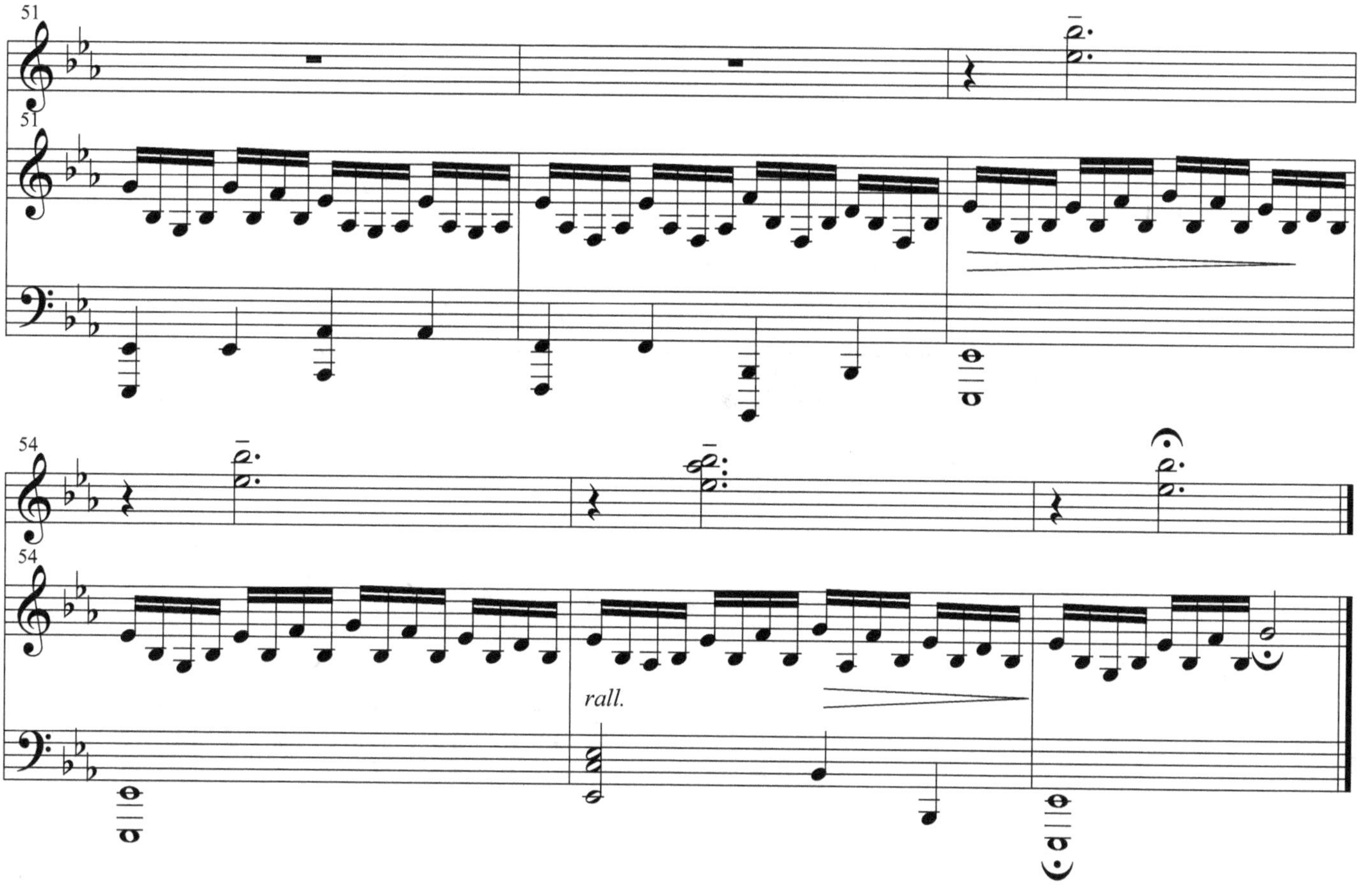
51
51
54
54
rall.

DUNGEON

Etude in G minor

Rebecca Belliston

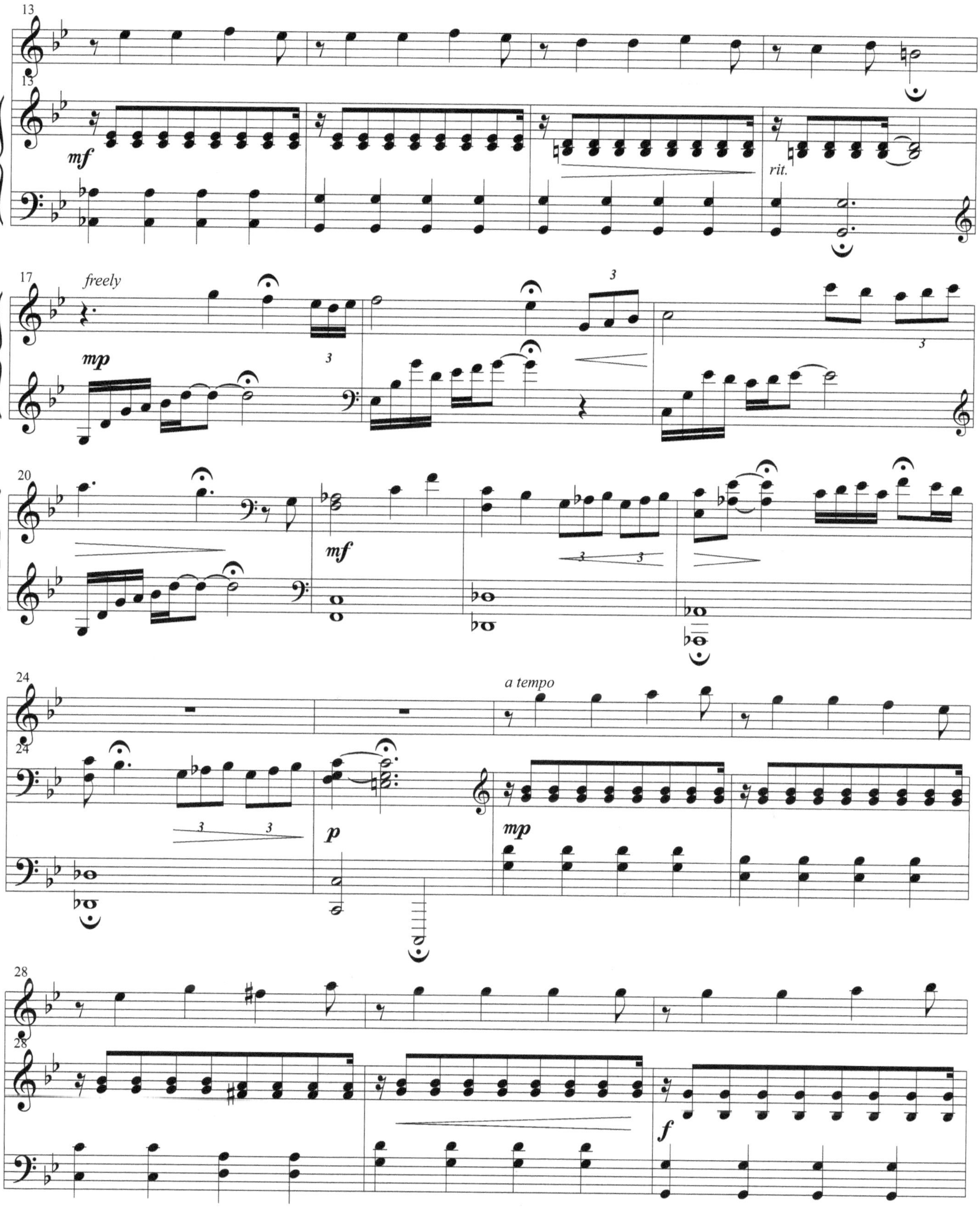
13
mf
rit.
17
freely
mp
20
mf
24
a tempo
p
mp
28
f

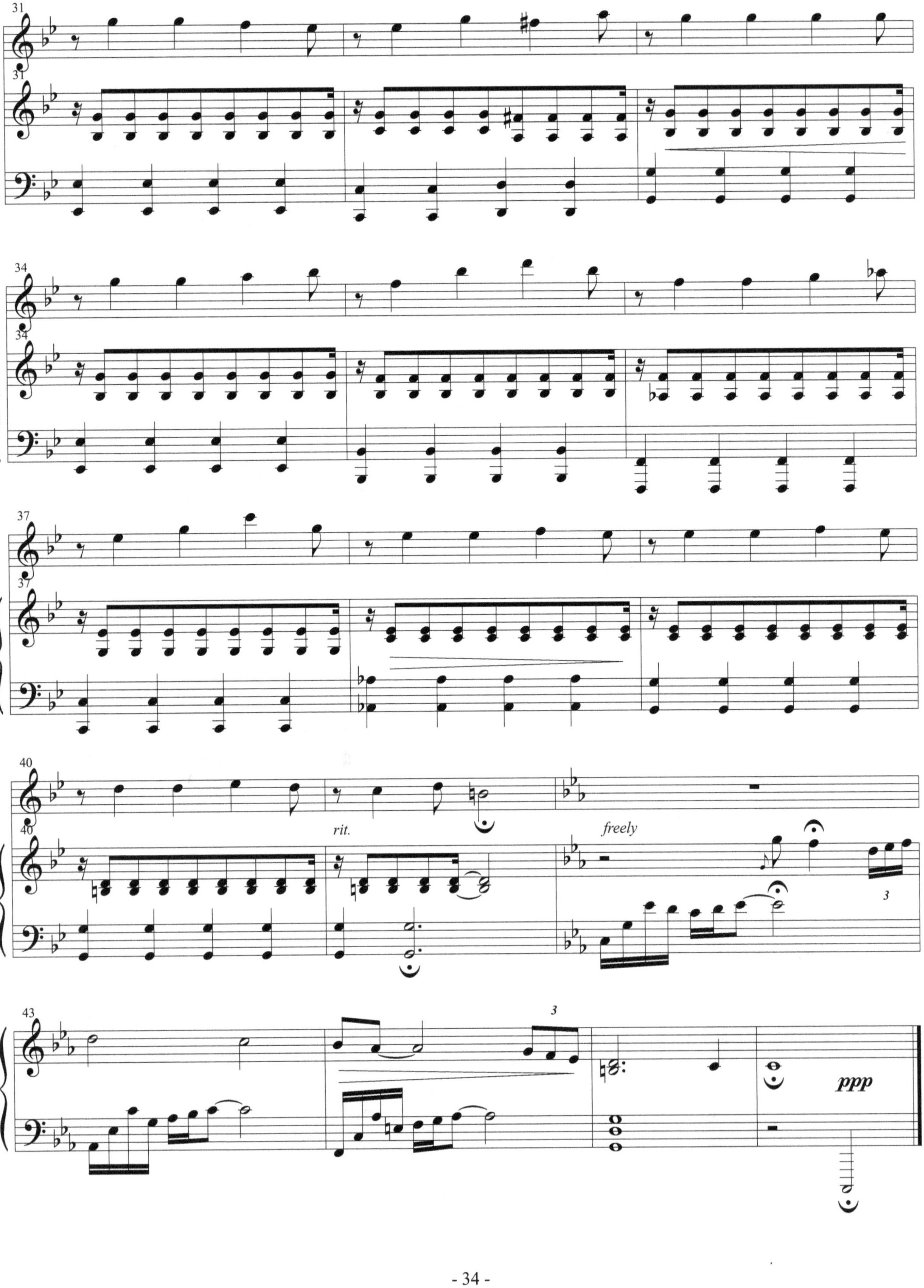
31
34
37
40
rit.
freely
3
43
3
ppp

CORONATION

Processional in G

Rebecca Belliston

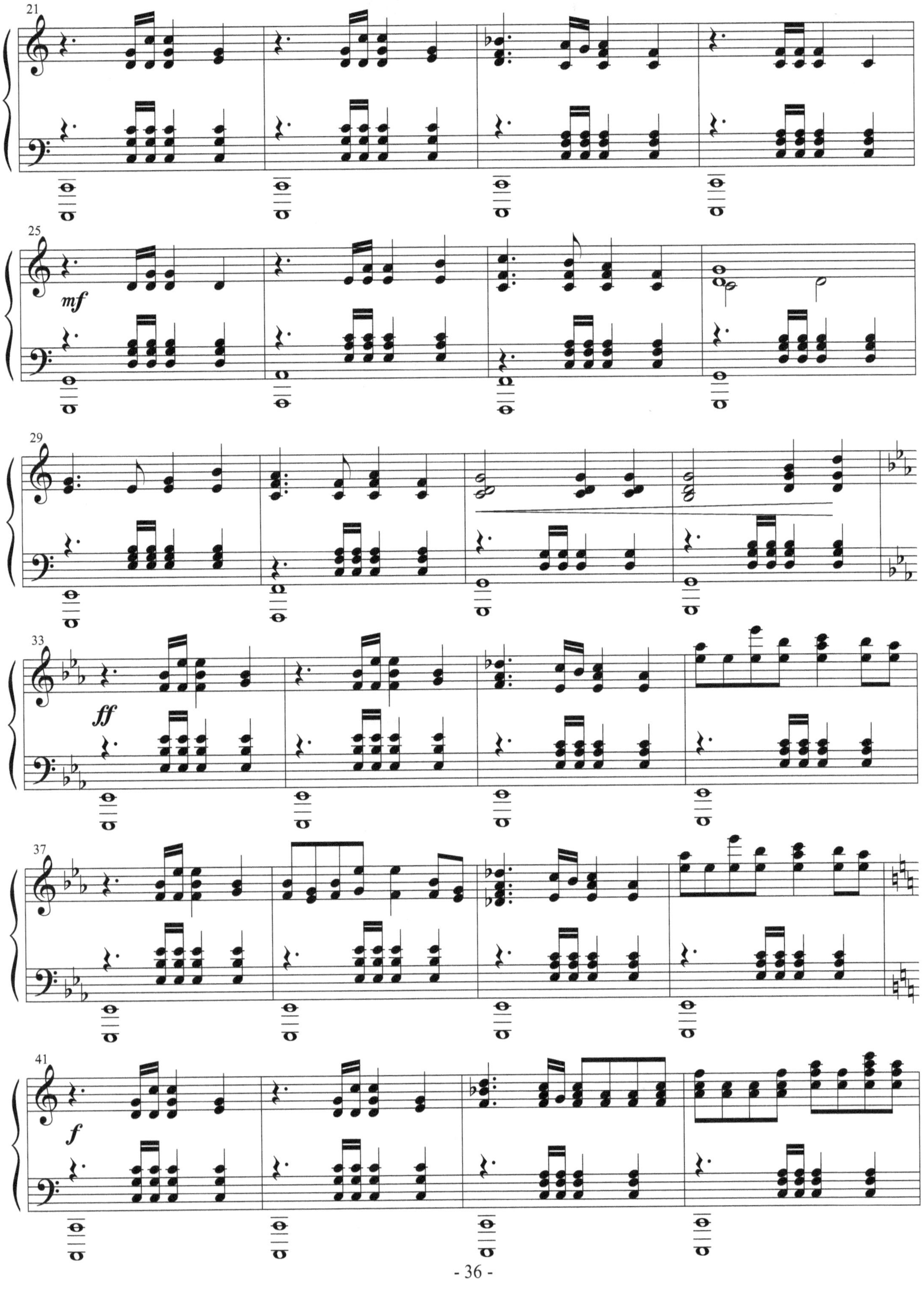
21
25
mf
29
33
ff
37
41
f

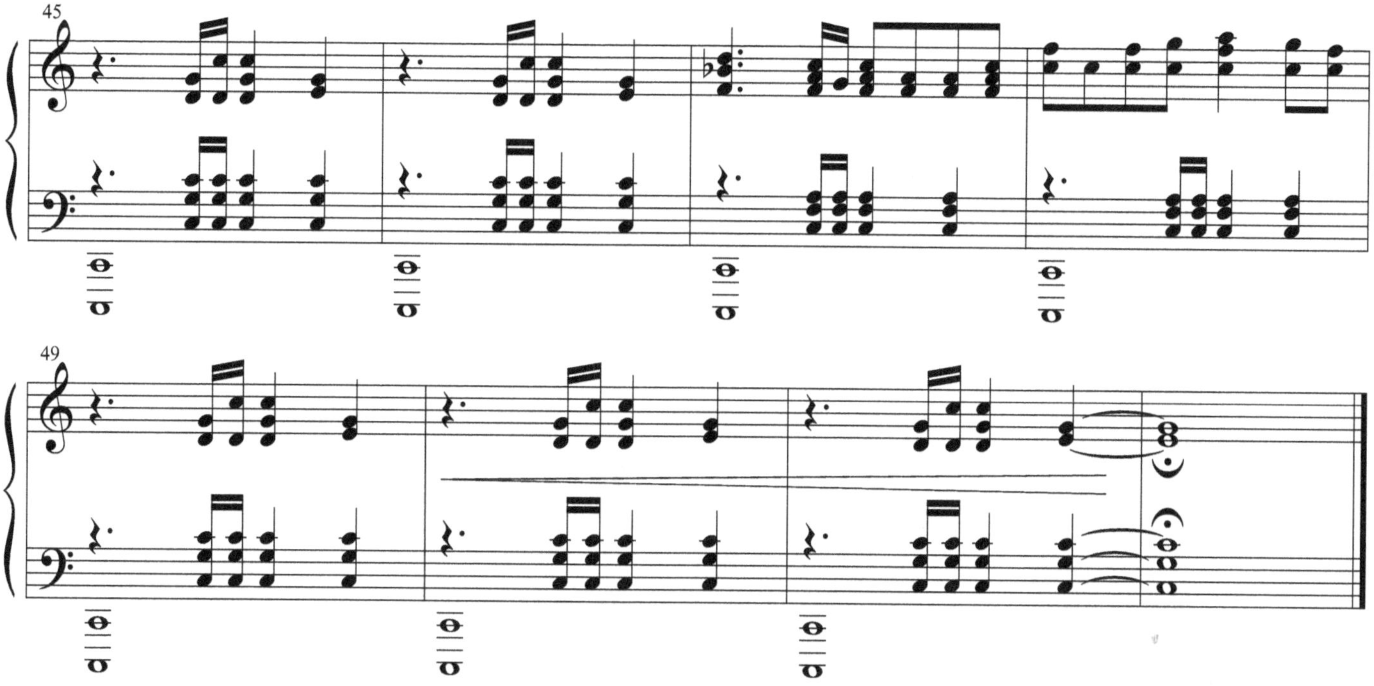
45
49

About the Composer

Rebecca Lund Belliston studied music and orchestration at Brigham Young University and Utah State University. She is the composer and arranger of over forty religious and classical-style songs, including the bestselling original Christmas choral work, "For There's a Savior Born." Rebecca is also the author of six novels, including the dystopian trilogy, *Citizens of Logan Pond.* When she's not writing books or music, she likes to curl up with a good book, play tennis, and make sarcastic comments—usually not at the same time. She lives in Michigan with her husband and five children.

Connect:

Website: rebeccabelliston.com
Facebook: @rebeccalundbelliston
Twitter: @rlbelliston
Instagram: @rebeccabelliston
Youtube: @rebeccabelliston
Subscribe: tinyurl.com/RLBSubscribe

REBECCA BELLISTON

Original Compositions & Arrangements

classical

Etude in Eb minor – Piano Solo
Fugue in C minor – Piano Solo
Fugue in F minor – Piano Duet
Heart of Red, Blood of Blue – Piano Solo Album
Jerusalem: Prelude in C minor – Piano Solo
Prelude in A – Piano Solo
Sonata in A minor – Piano Solo
Prelude in Bb minor – Piano Solo

contemporary / popular

A Whole New World – Big Note
Greatest Showman Songs – Big Note | Easy Piano
Look Past – Piano/Vocal/Guitar
My Country, 'Tis of Thee – Piano Solo

hymns / religious

A Poor Wayfaring Man of Grief – Piano Solo
Abide With Me; 'Tis Eventide – Piano Solo | Violin Solo
Come, and Be With Me – SATB
Come Unto Jesus – SATB Hymn
Feast Upon the Words of Christ – SSA
For the Love of Hymns – 6 LDS Hymn Arrangements for Solo Piano
How Great Thou Art – Vocal Solo | Vocal Duet | Piano Solo | Instrumental
I Will Make Weak Things Strong: Ether 12:27 – Men's Vocal Solo
Jesus, the Very Thought of Thee – Piano Solo
Nearer Medley – SA Duet
Nearer, Dear Savior, to Thee – SATB | Piano Solo | Violin Solo
Oil For Your Lamps – SSA
Oh, How Lovely Was the Morning – SATB | Piano Solo | Piano/Organ Duet
Still Be My Vision – SATB | SSA | Vocal Duet
We Come Unto Thy House, O Lord – SATB

christmas

Christmas Handbells for Children - Handbells
Come, Thou Long Expected Jesus – SATB
For There's a Savior Born – SATB
Noel: A Christmas Medley – SATB | Piano Solo
Oh, Come, All Ye Faithful – Piano Duet | SSATTB
Silent Night – SATB | Vocal Solo | Vocal Duet | Instrumental
Where Are You Christmas? – Big Note Piano

Complete listing at rebeccabelliston.com